Further Away Than Here

By George K. Karos II

ISBN: 978-93-6354-704-9

First Edition: 2024
Rs. 200/-

Cyberwit.net
HIG 45 Kaushambi Kunj, Kalindipuram
Allahabad - 211011 (U.P.) India
http://www.cyberwit.net
Tel: +(91) 9415091004
E-mail: info@cyberwit.net

Printed at Repro India Limited.

Contents

Integration as Whole

We are interconnected molecules
Sharing corresponding planes of realities
Contentiously adapting to shared spaces
Impacted by biospheres ripening restlessly
Alongside our loosely banded entropy.

Course in Time

Enacted systems controlling hypocrisies
establishing contingencies of forbearance
through each course in time intended.

Dormancy Domain

Potent harmonies align
within my perceptions
of nothing's daft supremacy
now, before, and sometime after
this poem's measured creation.

Viably Parallel

Together, attached,
sharing viably parallel lives
informed by current and past eras
that vanish to reappear, again.

Granted Peace

I am granted peace
when I become aware
of the immense beauty existing momentarily
with everything.

Awake for Now

Reacquainting oneself
formally
ritualistically transpiring
existence
alongside the dominion of
others.

More, and More Less Guided

Reason eclipsed by obstacles
allow relationships to ensue
between the monumental mysteries of life
and through poetry's comforting illusions
after generations of atomic reverberations
combine valiantly in translucent dream portals
to awaken nondescript shivering masses
accounting for births and rebirths of times to come.

Life: What are We Here For?

Life, what are we here for?
We must find a way
to answer this question
moment to moment
providing for ourselves
shelter and income
and the civility to pay debts

in between filling our stomachs

and those of fellow humans

with and without indifferences
now until the end of time.

Alone to Create

Constant alienation
confirms my alarming awareness
and directs this poem's enchanted creation.

Whichever Works

Flowing.
Interrupted.
Never struggling for answers.
Expanding efforts to understand
why I am confused about how sometimes
I cannot understand anything's understanding.

Reeling.
Exhausted.
Exasperated from chaos's surveillance
directing its oblivious recipients
into its spellbound patterns
marketed with mechanisms
to manipulate inclusion.

Convocation of Mayhem

Humanity exploits repetitions,
never-ending trepidations of sorted phases
offering a distinct awareness
that nothing matters but gratification
in disparate and reactive communities
lacking the human dignities
we have collectively created.

Designated Cosmoses

Timeless dynamisms communicate
through apportioned atmospheres
too near, or too far
from oneself
and all others.

The Return to a Distraught Place

I have arrived, again,
to a distraught place
where I am aware
of my hunger and homelessness
destined by fraudulent relations
imagined as safe spaces among deviants
awaiting the indefinite outcomes
of humanity's poor judgements.

Seeking Solutions

As you ignore
your individual relevance
and deny self-meaning,
you may possibly discover
unrivaled societal distress,
but you are never exempt
from the everchanging quest
to discover useful solutions.

Biography

Starting and ending
second upon second
in succession of years
for others to document
moment upon proximate moment.

Amnesty Groove

Amnesty grooves
enfold polite crevices
of our imaginations
to be learned or felt
by unborn generations
for years to come.

Amnesty grooves
commences or concludes
as modified truths
for those we have hurt
and those who've hurt
us in return.

Routine Labor

Trudging ahead of each undertaking
indisputably granted an agreement
to be compensated accordingly.

A Tough Year or So

A tough year, or so.
Positively prescient liberties
 of vast micro chasms
provide reprieve
from narcissistic preoccupations
predominantly functioning as social constructs
imposing its will upon whatever I happen to be.
A tough year, or so.

Continuous War and Murder

War and murder continue
never to be stopped
by either religion
or government peacekeeping
promoting tolerance
and goodwill deeds
as mourners lament
a killers' further actions
that ends the lives of loved ones.

Can You Feel Safe Now?

Can you feel safe now?

As you seek to organize
your conception of God
flowing unpredictably in your mind
like birds chirping enthusiastically
to impress upon you their alertness
inside changing environments introduced to you
in sequences of shared ongoing moments?

Can you feel safe now?

Suffering's Timeline

Suffering occurs
when it arrives and recurs

from birth, through life,
and while waiting death,

as an encountered omnipresence
set free to reappear in rubrics of time.

Savory Notions

Benevolent memories
become experiences
safely reposed
in history.

Anxiety Exists

Anxiety exists unceasingly
circulating through realms
of consumptive environments
depriving those lacking income,
and those so frequently forgotten.

Veracity

Selfishly obsessed
with their own certainty,
people disallow truth's
verifiable authenticities.
Accepting truth prolongs your brief
conceptions of existence.

Let Words Root into Thoughts

Let your words root
into thoughts
where they become something
other than amplifications of sounds.
Let your words root
into your thoughts

where utterances transport redemptive potencies
that fashion harmonies to welcome suitable outcomes.

Traumatic Tenure

Absorbing my fleeting existence
aggressively annihilated
within detached determinants
trying to win my composed
conscience.

Felonious Feats

The lawlessly insane
thoughtlessly sanction anger
and impulsively annihilate peace
to substitute their terror.

Lied About

Disaffected. Misrepresented.
Suffering the outcome
of a false accusation.
Someone lied about me.

Onlookers never helped my vindication.
Envious and greedy people
capable of great atrocities
are sometimes nudged by kindness.

Attention Diverted

I am fortunate to own a pair of glasses
that allowed me to observe an early night,
as a remarkable sky's salt and peppered clouds
travelled fiercely and fluctuating -
either fixed, or in unison -
decelerating my consciousness
and inviting me to ruminate
as pending darkness overcame my view.

Father Forgiven

I have forgiven my father
who neglected me often,
an absent custodian to his only son,
the boy metamorphosed into a man,
allowing this restorative poem
to be healingly written.

Being Conscientious

Rapidly respiring
Beyond easily existing
until nuanced sorrows
are guided by joys
present in every moment.

Further Away Than Here

Nobody can listen
long enough to hear
the ephemeral exultations
of the humbled and distressed
perpetually weeping in distances
experienced further away than here.

Our Joint Claims to the Cosmos

I sense we are together.
Plasma forms galaxies
manifesting universe
we now call years.
Hydrogen forms frequencies
of light manifesting existence
contained by gravity's pull
creating carbon release
contributing to atmospheres
unearthed enduringly
for phenomenon evolving
into spectra's standards.

Situations Revealed

The familiarity of distortion
coexists with measurable encounters
renewing opportunities revealed to me
in every discernibly wakeful moment.

Derivations of Discontents

Discontents may arise
in repetitive patterns
shouldering myopic wits
of faithful standards
omnipresent as epiphanies
either appearing, or disappearing
to reveal God's light within me.

The Coldness of Age

With age, many of us turn inward.
A definite lack of feeling overtakes us.
No one really listens to anyone accept those they can control or manage.
Coldly, many reject the kindness of others.
Misinterpreting warm gestures as unconfident actions.
Sadly, many embrace what best benefits us.
We welcome only what profits our self-interests.
With age many of us turn inward.
A definite lack of feeling overtakes us.

Ceaseless Disconnection

Agitated chatter and texts
via electronic devices
redirect collective concerns
enhancing distractions to wellness.

Exploring Myself

Wise old and versed
the ways of departure
yielding, uniting,
and gracefully abounding
relinquishing control
the need to manage,
willfully pardoned
and seeking redemption.
Welcomed assertions
of kind calibrations
detained or contained
for now, and evermore.
Transient mercy
floating contagious
above and beyond
mortal coil.
Cared for, abandoned,
the cycles of life
informing my behavior,
shedding light on my strife.

Presence Unsurpassed

Surviving years upon decades
with redundant feelings of inadequacies
trembling forthright and forever uncertain
of generational atmospheres forced into submission
by egotistic cultural authorities
derived from relations formed through circumstances
lacking perpetual goodwill.

Dynasties Last

Dynasties last until they expire
threatened by withdrawals
of weakening aspirations
where brassy bold trumpets
no longer sound for persons
previously considered important.

Saving a Dollar Bill

Saving a dollar bill
With the spirited intention
Of planning for future needs
Or in circumstances intended
When cash is depleted and debits due,
Where everything we thought we needed
Would add up and be paid for.

Questioning the Origins of Me

The notion I was born
after living inside another person
is an incomprehensible conundrum
contributing to my magnificent confusion.

Abandoning Myself

Self-desertion is masked irresponsibility
for not becoming accountable for me.

An Appetite for Refuge

I have always sought refuge
in countless conditions
where knowing myself
always determined
an appropriate response.

Weather Conditions

Temperatures waver
in circumstances
where weather conditions
pilot precipitation.

Remembering Joys

Remembering joys
enables me to exist more freely
from debilitating standards
discriminant of my heart's fitness.

Whatever I May Be

Whatever I may be
is clearer to me
when I mutely listen
and coexist within
the confines of heart and mind
I perceive as an invitation
to unfailingly subsist.

Terrifically Still

Wind wallops voraciously
outside my rented room's window
as I lay terrifically still
on an air mattress.
I am neither fearful
nor desiring
anything
but now.

www.ingramcontent.com/pod-product-compliance
Lightning Source LLC
LaVergne TN
LVHW041000150826
845672LV00002B/787

* 9 7 8 9 3 6 3 5 4 7 0 4 9 *